Copyright & Disclaimer

Travel Like A Local (Map Book) By Maxwell Fox (2019)

Map Created on Inkatlas.com.

Copyright OpenStreetMap contributors (openstreetmap.org), Inkatlas.

OpenStreetMap data incl. legend/map key is based on CC-BY-SA license.

Travel Planner & Lined Paper Pages by ShastaCrafts.

The information and images contained in this book, for example cover art, is protected under all Federal and International Copyright Laws and Treaties. Therefore, any use or reprint of the material in the book, either paperback or electronic, is prohibited. Users may not transmit or reproduce the material in any way shape or form – mechanically or electronically such as recording, photocopying or information storage and retrieval system – without getting prior written permission from the publisher/author.

All attempts have been made to verify the information contained in this book, but the author and publisher do not bear any responsibility for errors or omissions. Any perceived negative connotation of any individual, group, or company is purely unintentional. Furthermore, this book is intended as entertainment only and as such, any and all responsibility for actions taken by reading this book lies with the reader alone and not with the author or publisher. This book is not intended as medical, legal, or business advice and the reader alone holds sole responsibility for any consequences of any actions taken after reading this book. Additionally, it is the reader's responsibility alone and not the author's or publisher's to ensure that all applicable laws and regulations for the business practice are adhered to.

About Maxwell Fox

With a taste for adventure, Maxwell Fox has always been passionate about one thing: traveling.

Ever since he was a little boy he was filled with a unique curiosity and an adventurous spirit that took him along to beautiful and amazing new experiences. From short trips with family to imaginary travels around the world, his wanderlust was his driving force from a young age.

He was fascinated by the endless possibilities of new lands, people and ways of life and that is exactly what he looked to discover every time he went on a new adventure.

From trying the local cuisine and exploring brand new flavors, to visiting all the important cultural and historical sights, he carefully planned each trip so he could experience each place to the fullest and discover every little corner.

What he was after was not the tourist experience but the unique immersion into a new community and a different culture.

So what he did was strive to experience each city like a true local.

Traveling gave him the opportunity to increase his knowledge and interest in history, culture, art, architecture and language. Through his experiences he sought to improve his skills and become the best version of himself.

After his many adventures and life changing experiences, he tried to find a path that would excite him just as much as traveling did.

So he thought of what travelers everywhere have in common and what thing brings all his interests together. And that's how he started his journey through the artful science of cartography.

With a formal training in cartography and a unique love for traveling and adventure, Maxwell Fox decided to make it his life's mission to help fellow travelers around the world have the most amazing experience every time they travel.

ACCOMMODATION

 Hotel
 Motel
 Hostel
 Camping

FOOD & DRINK

 Restaurant
 Fast food
 Cafe
 Ice cream
 Bar
 Pub

SHOP & SERVICE

 Supermarket
 Depertment store
 Marketplace
 Kiosk
 Greengrocer
 Alcohol
 Confectionery
 Bakery
 Tea
 Electronics
 Computer
 Mobile
 Hifi
Clothes
Shoes

 Jewellery
 Bag
 Beauty
 Perfumery
 Hairdresser
 Laundry
 Travel agency
 Books
 Art
 Gift
 Toys
 Florist

TRANSPORTATION

 Parking
 Taxi
 Bus stop
 Bus station
 Subway entrance
 Rental car
 Fuel
 Charging station
 Rental bicycle
 Aerodrome
 Helipad
 Ferry

ENTERTAINMENT, ARTS & CULTURE

 Cinema
 Theatre

♪	Nightclub		**LAND USE**
🏛	Museum	▬▬▬	Highway
📖	Library	▬▬▬	Primary road
♀	Artwork	▬▬▬	Secondary road
🎨	Arts Center	▬▬▬	Tertiary road
⛲	Fountain	▬▬▬	Unclassifield road
✳	Viewpoint	▬▬▬	Railway
		▬▬▬	Tram railway
	FINANCIAL	▬ ▬ ▬	Ferry road
🏧	Atm	▬▬▬	Water
💵	Bank	▬▬▬	Beach
		▲	Volcano
	ACTIVITY	▬▬▬	Border
🏃	Fitness	▬▬▬	Quarry
🏊	Swimming	▬▬▬	Comemercial
🏌	Golf	▬▬▬	Nature
	Miniature golf	▬▬▬	Park
	Playground	▬▬▬	Residential area
	HEALTHCARE		**OTHER**
⊕	Hospital	i	Information
	Doctor	🚻	Toilets
	Pharmacy	🗑	Waste basket
🦷	Dentist		Drinking water
👓	Optician		Table
			Bench
	POST	[↕]	Elevator
✉	Post box		Police
	Post office	🔥	Fire station
		⚖	Courthouse
		🚩	Embassy

Map of Londonderry (United Kingdom)

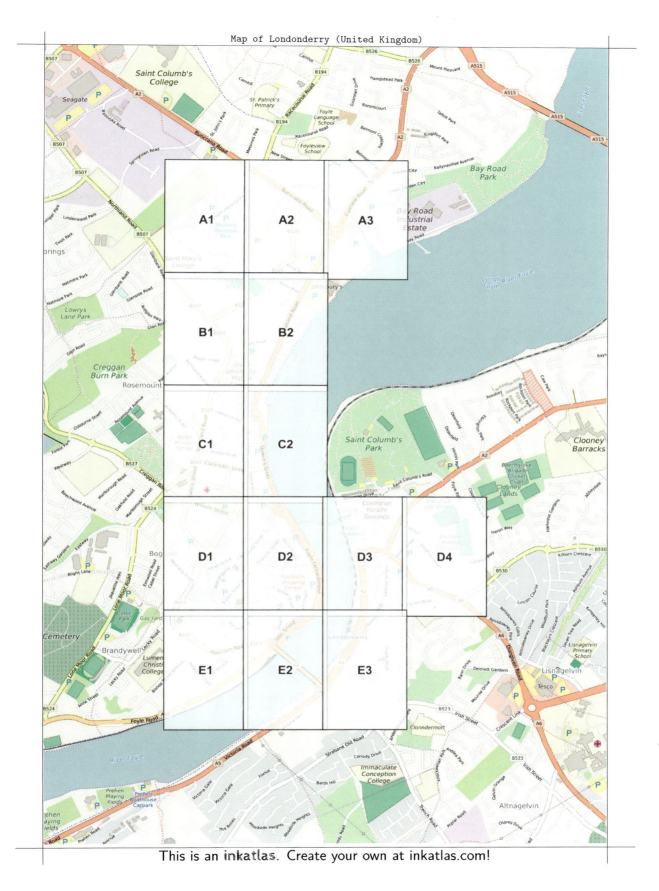

This is an inkatlas. Create your own at inkatlas.com!

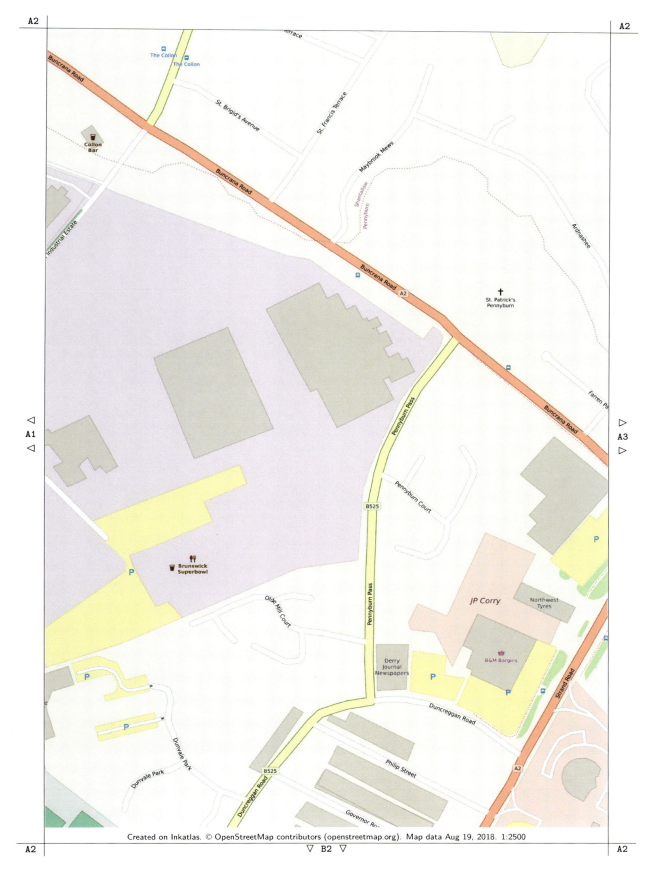

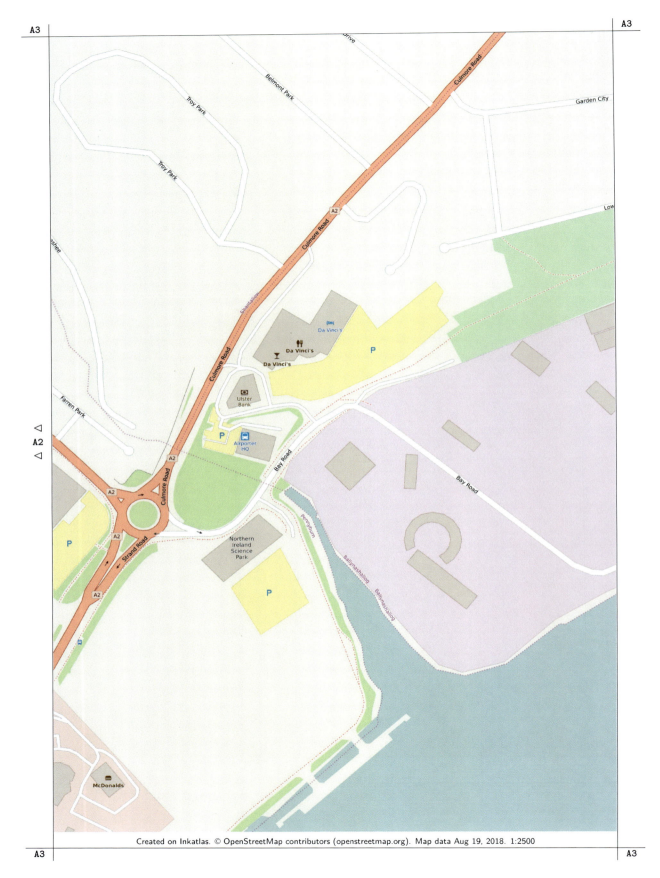

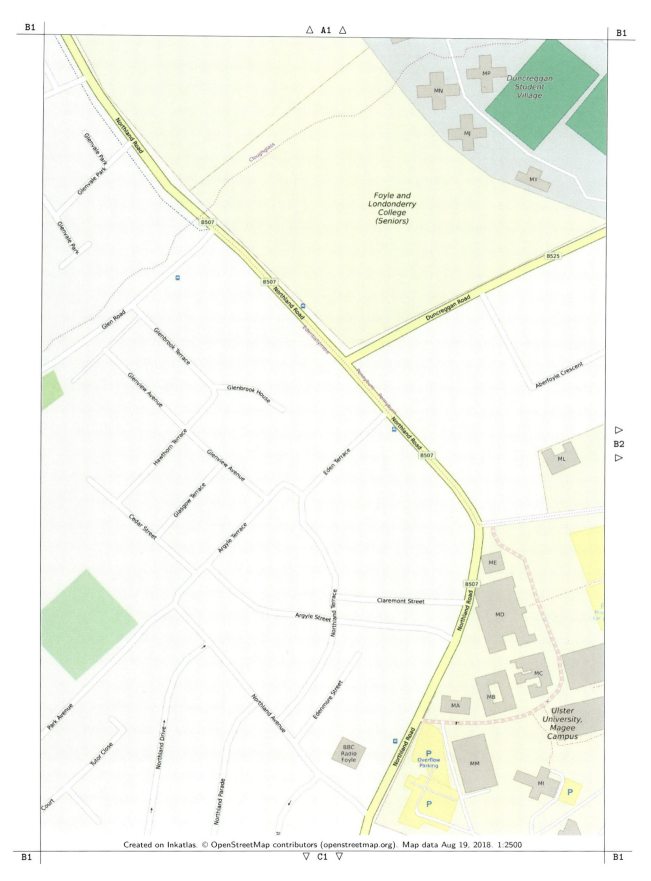

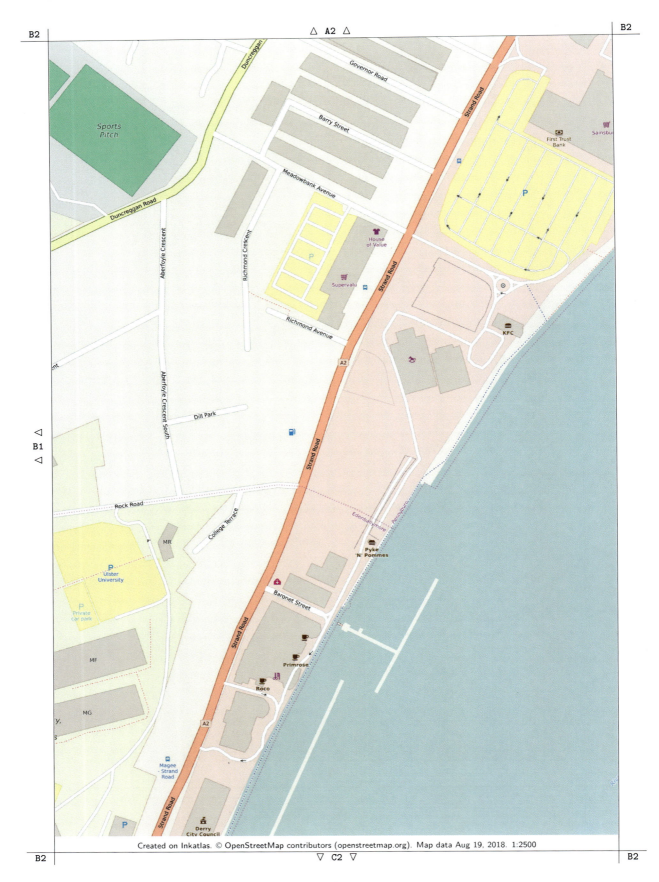

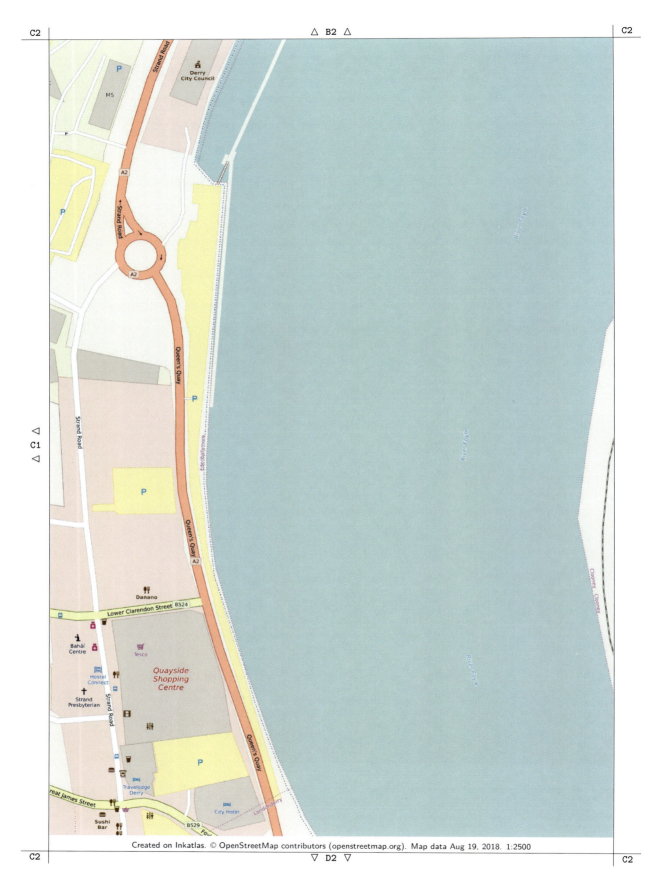

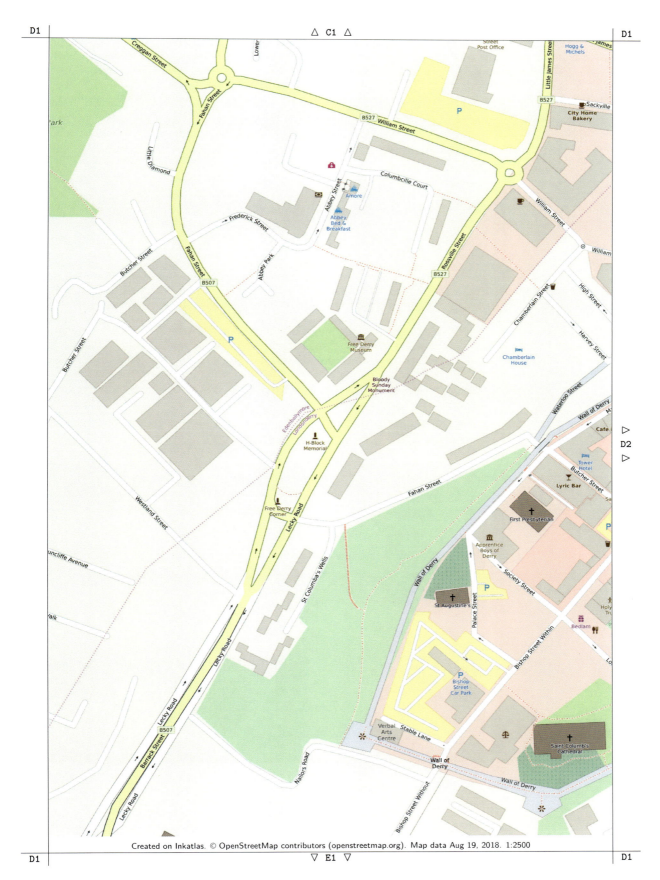

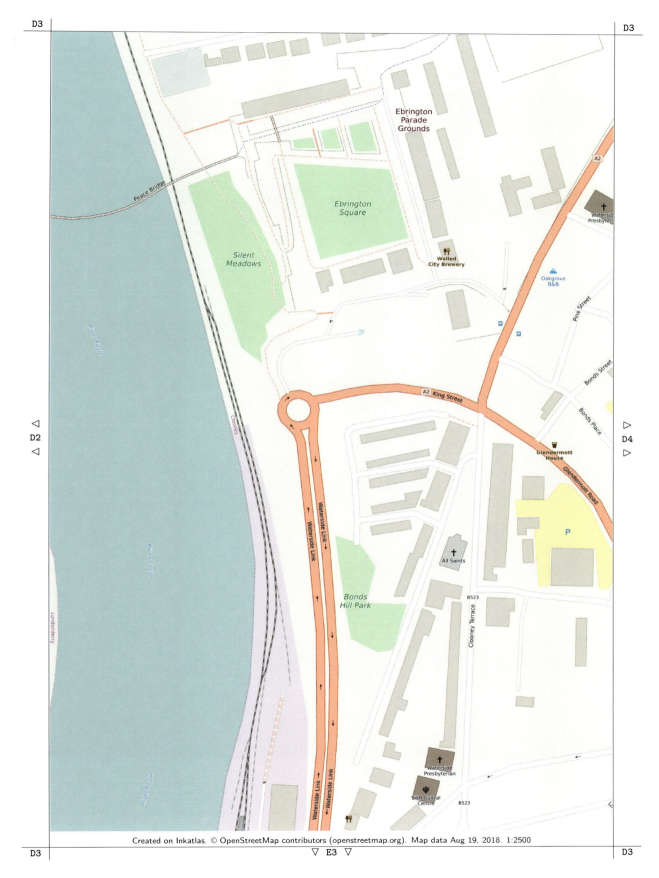

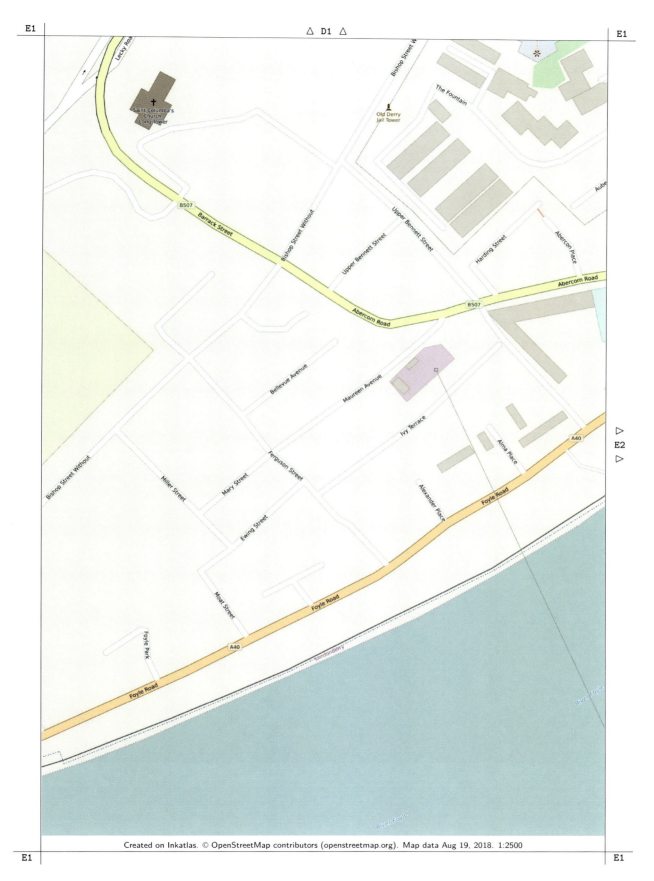

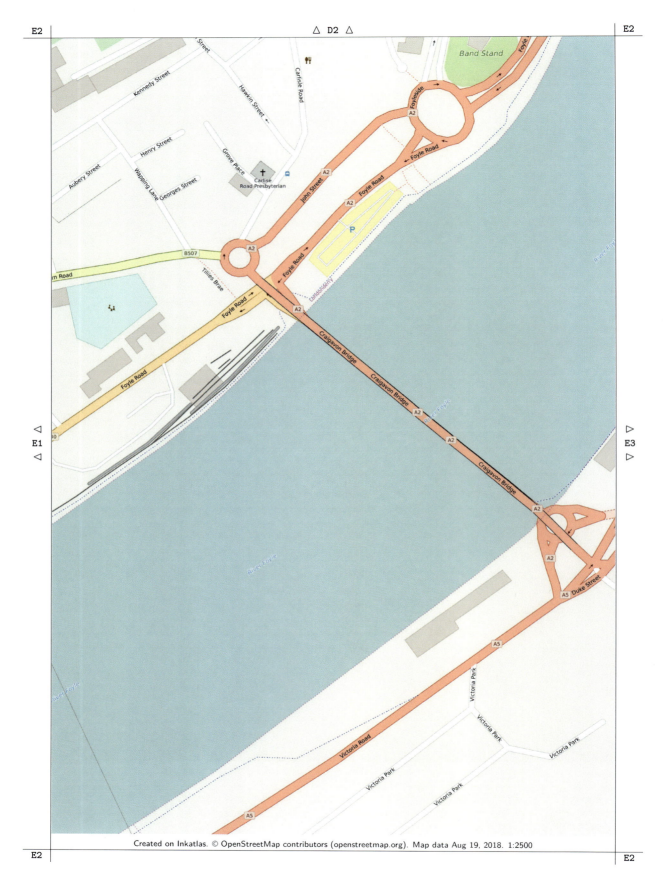

Travel Planner

WHERE?

WHEN?

FROM: ___/___/___
TO: ___/___/___
DAYS: _____

TRANSPORTATION

☐ ✈ ☐ 🚌 ☐ 🚗 ☐ 🚤 ☐ 🚲 ☐ 🚶 ☐ _____

DETAILS:

Printed in Great Britain
by Amazon